Easy Coconut Flour Recipes

Healthy Recipes for Breakfast, Lunch & Dinner

Cyrille Malet

Sign-up for Free eBooks : type http://bit.ly/14oc3FG

What You Get If You Subscribe :

*Free eBooks and Discounts

*Latest News, New Releases, Updates

*Exclusive Content (Free Recipes, Additional Content Only Available Here)

*Just Goodies, No spam - ever

Sign-up NOW : http://bit.ly/14oc3FG

Any question ?

Like us // on Facebook

Follow us // on twitter.com/lesartistesm

Contact us // lesartistesbooks@gmail.com

Table of Contents

Introduction

Are you missing foods made of wheat flour ever since identifying a gluten intolerance or starting a gluten free diet? Coconut Flour is a perfect substitute for people who just love coconut, want a healthier flour option, have restricted their diet or a have sensitivity to wheat. Using coconut flour, you can enjoy your favorite breads, muffins, biscuits, and desserts without suffering from the digestive irritation that many people experience.

Why Coconut Flour is Healthier

Coconut flour has less calories and more health benefits; great for low carbohydrate or Paleo diets. It is made from drying and finely grinding the coconut meat that is left over from the production of coconut milk.

This flour is considered a slow-carbohydrate with a high dietary fiber content. Approximately **60% of its composition is non-digestible fiber.** This fiber has no caloric count and cannot be digested by your body, which results in cleaning out of the digestion system, eliminating toxins and regulating of digestion. The remaining portion of the coconut flour composition offers **14% coconut oil, made up of polyunsaturated, monounsaturated and saturated fats.** The majority of the fats are short and medium-chain fats which are sent directly to the liver for energy production. This saves energy because no enzymes are needed for digestion. The remaining components of the flour are **20% protein and 8% digestible carbohydrates.** Coconut also contains lauric acid that offers benefits of **boosting the immune system** and manganese which helps your body to absorb nutrients.

Coconut Flour Vs Other Flours

So, how does coconut compare to other flours? It contains less carbohydrates than other nut and wheat flours, equal protein to whole wheat flour, and more fiber than other nut flours. On the other side, it is a bit more expensive than wheat flours and contains less protein than other nut flours, such as almond. When using coconut flour, the coconut taste is distinguishable than in other nut or wheat flours. This can be an advantage when baking recipes that are complimented by coconut flavor. Coconut flour can withstand higher temperatures than almond flour. Almond flour recipes baking temperature usually falls between 300 and 325 degrees, while **coconut flour can be baked in temperatures up to 350 degrees without burning.** The last aspect is ease of cooking.

How To Cook Coconut Flour Easily

Coconut flour is very dry and absorbs a lot of moisture. In order to achieve a moist result, the recipes require a high ratio of eggs to flour. It is recommended that **for every 1 cup of coconut flour, you include six beaten eggs.** When substituting coconut flour for wheat flour in baked goods, it is recommended that you **use 1 cup of wheat flour to ¼ cup coconut flour.** A small amount of coconut flour also goes a long way and creates a thick consistency. It must be beaten very well to avoid a grainy consistency. A solution to clumping is to soak the flour in liquids for 15 minutes prior to preparing. It behaves very differently than wheat flour or nut flours because of its high absorbency.

How To Combine Coconut Flour With Other Flours

There are other gluten free flours that compliment coconut flour well in recipes. One you will find in this book is **quinoa flour**. Quinoa is made from ground up seeds from the quinoa plant and gives a nutty flavor. It also has a very high protein content of about 18%. This flour has an approximate 1 cup: 1 cup wheat flour ratio but also requires more eggs to keep it bound together. **Garbanzo flour** is another protein-rich flour that can be used at a 7/8: 1 cup ratio to wheat flour. It is rich in fiber and calcium and works great in non-sweet recipes like pizza, breads and spice cakes. It can have a distinct flavor that shows through, so partners well in smaller amounts mixed with coconut flour.

Almond flour has a ratio of approximately ½ cup to 1 cup wheat flour when baking in recipes. It has a higher fat content, is less dense and weighs less than wheat flour, so baked goods come out a bit different texture wise. Substituting alternative flours in place of wheat flour can be tricky and take experimentation. You can also save on ingredients and leave the experimenting to other people by using recipes specifically for the flour of your choice, which you can find in this book!

Are you ready to try some recipes? You can find coconut flour at your local health food store, online or at organic grocery stores. Raw organic coconut flour is recommended and some popular brands are Bob's Red Mill, Tropical Traditions or Wilderness Family Naturals. You will find a collection of delicious recipes below for you to experiment and enjoy your new flour!

The Recipes

I Coconut Flour Recipes (With Agave Syrup)

Pancakes

1/2 c. coconut flour
4 eggs
1 c. milk
2 tsp. vanilla extract
1 tbsp. agave syrup
1 tsp. baking soda
1/2 tsp. salt
Butter for frying

Delicious Sunday morning pancakes without the hang over. Start by heating up a greased pan over low-med heat. You will need two bowls. In the first combine the wet ingredients including eggs, milk, agave and vanilla. In the second bowl combine the flour, baking soda and salt. Next mix one mixture into the other and whisk until the lumps dissolve completely. Pour the batter into the pan and cook until one side starts to brown, then flip and brown the other side. After that the delicious pancakes are ready for the toppings of your choice. Fresh fruit is a delicious choice that won't spoil your healthy efforts!

Donut Holes

5 tbsp. coconut flour
1 egg
1/4 c. butter
1/4 c. sugar
1/8 tsp. salt
1/4 tsp. vanilla extract
1/2 c. confectioners' sugar (optional)

Heat your oven up to 350 degrees and grease a baking sheet. Combine together the butter, sugar and vanilla until well mixed, then whisk in the egg. Mix in coconut flour and salt well. Roll the dough into balls and line them up on your baking sheet. Bake until they turn golden, for about 15 minutes. After they are baked and cooled, sprinkle them with confectioner's sugar if desired.

Banana Bread Muffins

1/2 c. coconut flour
5 eggs
2 bananas
1 tbsp. agave syrup
1/4 c. coconut oil or butter
1 tsp. baking soda
1 tsp. vanilla
Small amount of milk

Preheat your oven to 400 degrees. While you oven is heating up mix all ingredients in a medium sized bowl. Use a whisk or immersion blender to mix until smooth. You can thin the batter with a little milk if needed. The batter should be somewhat thick. Pour batter evenly into greased muffin tins and bake for 13-18 minutes until lightly browned in the middle.

Blueberry Muffins

1/4 c. sifted coconut flour
1/4 tsp. baking powder
3 large eggs
3 tbsp. melted butter
3 tbsp. agave syrup
1/4 tsp. vanilla and salt
3/4 cup of blueberries

These muffins are all the blueberry goodness and none of the bloated tummy. Start by heating your oven to 400 degrees. Next you will combine the flour and baking powder until thoroughly combined. In a separate bowl combine well the butter, agave, vanilla and eggs. Once mixed well add the flour mixture to the wet ingredients and whisk until all lumps are dissolved. Fold in the blueberries. Now pour into cupcake liners in a muffin pan, filling them about half way. Bake them for 16 minutes and poke with a toothpick to check if any batter sticks. If it comes out clean they are ready.

Apple Cinnamon Muffins

1/2 cup coconut flour
5 eggs
1 cup applesauce
2-3 tbsp. cinnamon
1 tsp. baking soda
1 tsp. vanilla
2 tsp. agave syrup
1/4 cup coconut oil

Preheat your oven to 400 degrees. Mix all the ingredients except agave syrup in a medium sized bowl until well mixed. Let the batter sit for 5 minutes and grease a muffin pan with your coconut oil. Use 1/3 cup measure to spoon into muffin tins then bake for 12-15 minutes. They should start to brown and not be soft when lightly touched on top. Let theses cool down for 2 minutes and drizzle with agave syrup if you desire, then serve.

Cream Cheese Cake

1/2 c. coconut flour
6 large eggs
3 tbsp. butter

1/2 c. yogurt
1/4 c. agave syrup
1/2 tsp. baking soda
1/4 tsp. salt
1/4 c. chopped pecans
1 tsp. cinnamon
1 tbsp. agave syrup
1 tbsp. coconut flour

Fill:
8 oz. cream cheese
1 large egg
2 tsp. agave syrup

Heat your oven to 325 degrees and grease an 8 inch round pan. Combine together cream cheese, 1 egg and agave syrup and save for later. Next in a separate bowl combine flour, eggs, butter, yogurt and syrup. Pour the mixture into the 8 inch pan and sprinkle chopped pecans throughout. Pour the filling over and use a knife to swirl it throughout. Bake for 25 minutes and then let it cool.

Sliced Bread

3/4 c. coconut flour
6 medium eggs
1/2 c. melted butter
1 tbsp. agave
1/4 tsp. salt
1 tsp. baking soda

Preheat your oven to 350 degrees. Beat the eggs well then add the butter, coconut flour, baking soda, agave and salt. Whisk thoroughly until all lumps have been worked out. Pour batter in a small loaf pan and bake for 25 minutes. Slice and enjoy!

Granola Bars

1/2 c. coconut flour
3 eggs
2 tbsp. coconut oil
1 c. almonds (chopped)
1/2 c. raisins
1/2 c. dates (chopped)
1 tsp. cinnamon
1/3 c. agave
3 tbsp. water
1/2 c. coconut shredded

Heat up your oven to 350 degrees and grease a pan. (9 x 13)
Combine the flour, almonds, raisins, dates, cinnamon, and coconut. Once these are combined well add the eggs, oil, agave and water. Pour mixture into the food processor and process to your desired consistency. Next, pour the mixture into the greased pan and compress it down using a spatula with water on it. Bake for 18 minutes when the edges will begin to turn brown.

Red Velvet Cupcakes

1/2 c. coconut flour
4 eggs
1/2 c agave syrup
2 tbsp. grape seed oil
2 1/2 tbsp. cocoa powdered unsweetened
1/4 tsp. salt and baking soda
1 tbsp. food color

Here is a healthy spin on the popular red velvet dessert. Start by heating your oven up to 350 degrees. Combine your flour, cocoa powder, salt and baking soda and mix well. In a separate bowl combine eggs, agave, grape seed oil and food coloring. Mix together the two combinations until all lumps have dissolved. Line a muffin pan with cupcake liners and fill about half way. Bake for about 20 minutes. You can test with a toothpick, they are done when nothing sticks to the toothpick.

German Chocolate Cupcakes with Pecan and Coconut Frosting

1/2 c. coconut flour
4 eggs
1/4 c. cacao powder
2 tbsp. grape seed oil
1 tsp. salt and baking soda
1 tbsp. vanilla

Frosting:
1/2 c coconut milk
1/2 c agave nectar
2 1/2 tsp. arrowroot powder
1/2 tbsp. water
3/4 c. coconut oil
3/4 c. finely processed pecans
3/4 cup coconut shredded and unsweetened

Heat your oven to 350 degrees

Heat a saucepan over med. and combine milk, salt and agave for about 8 minutes. Combine arrowroot powder and water in a separate container to make a well blended paste. Mix the paste into the milk mixture, combine rapidly and increase heat to high until the mixture boils. Take the pan off of the heat a slowly mix in the coconut oil. After this the mixture goes into the freezer for 25 minutes where it will turn solid and white. After 25 minutes remove and stir rapidly. The filling will become fluffy and then fold in the coconut and pecans. Set aside.

In a medium bowl sift the flour, baking soda, salt and cacao well. Then in a separate bowl combine eggs, oil, agave and vanilla. Next combine the egg mixture into the flour mixture and whisk until the lumps dissolve. Line a muffin pan with cupcake liners and fill them 1/2 of the way. Bake for about 20 minutes then remove, let cool and frost with filling.

II Coconut Flour Recipes (Without Agave Syrup)

Bacon Biscuits

3/4 c. coconut flour
5 eggs
1/2 tsp. salt
1 tsp. baking soda
1 tbsp. apple cider vinegar
1/2 c. vegetable shortening
4 slices crumbled
1/2 c. minced shallot

Heat your oven to 350 degrees and prepare a baking sheet with parchment paper. Start with a medium sized pan and fry the bacon, then remove bacon slices and crumble them. Leave the bacon fat in the pan and add the minced shallots. Sauté the shallots until soft then remove from pan and let cool. In a bowl sift together the flour, salt and baking soda. In a separate bowl whisk together 5 eggs and apple cider vinegar. Once well combined, mix the flour mixture in and beat until smooth and thick. Next you will mix until well combined the bacon, shallots and vegetable shortening. Spoon the mixture onto a baking sheet and make 12 biscuits. Bake for 15 minutes then enjoy!

Crepes

2 tbsp. coconut flour, sifted
1/4 tsp. vanilla extract
1/8 tsp. salt
2 eggs
2 tbsp. melted coconut oil
1/3 c. of whole milk
Pinch of nutmeg
Pinch of cinnamon

Start with a medium sized bowl and beat together the oil, eggs, vanilla and salt with a wire whisk. Mix in the coconut flour, cinnamon and nutmeg followed by the milk. Heat a skillet that's at least 8 inches in diameter over medium heat. When it is hot, melt the coconut oil in the pan. Now it is time to make your crepe! Pour 1/8 cup of batter in the skillet and swirl into a thin layer that covers the bottom of the pan to about 6 inches. Cook for about 1-2 minutes, you want the batter to get bubbly and cooked around the edges, then flip. Cook on the other side for 1-2 minutes more.

You can fill the crepes with your favorite topping. Berries are delicious, with a little whipped cream and a light dusting of coconut flour.

Spinach Soufflé

1 tbsp. coconut flour
3 large eggs
1c. cottage cheese
3 tbsp. butter
1 c. shredded cheddar cheese
10 oz. spinach

Heat up your oven to 350 degrees and grease a loaf pan. In a large bowl mix together the flour, oil, eggs, cottage cheese and then the cheese and spinach. Mix well and pour into loaf pan and bake until the top is golden brown.

Chicken Fingers

1/4 c. coconut flour
4 chicken breasts
3 egg whites
3/4 c. parmesan cheese

1/4 tsp. salt
Dash of pepper

Preheat oven to 200 degrees and heat a skillet to 375 degrees and fill with 2 inches of oil (we recommend coconut). Combine together cheese, flour, salt and pepper and mix well. In a separate bowl combine the egg whites and beat well. Take each piece of chicken and dip into the egg, then coat in the flour mixture. Then put the chicken into the oil and cook for about 2 minutes, then flip over and cook about 2 more minutes. You can cook about 4 at a time. Dry with a paper towel and keep them warm in the oven.

Coconut Shrimp

1/2 c. coconut flour
1/2 c. water
2 large eggs
1/4 c. corn starch
1 lb. peeled shrimp
1/2 tsp. salt
2 1/2 c. coconut shredded
1/2 c. coconut oil
1/2 c. palm oil

Heat the oils in a frying pan to 375 degrees. Combine and mix well the flour, salt, starch, water and eggs. Put the coconut onto a plate. Dip each shrimp into the egg mixture and then coat in coconut. Then place each shrimp in the frying pan for 1 minute, then flip over and fry one additional minute. Soak up some of the oil in a paper towel and serve.

III Coconut and Other Flour Recipes (With Agave Syrup)

Cinnamon Raisin Bread

1/4 c. coconut flour
2 large eggs
1 egg white
2 tbsp. butter
1/2 c. almond milk
2 tbsp. garbanzo flour
1 tbsp. quinoa flour
3 tbsp. flax meal
1 tsp. baking powder
1/4 tsp. salt
1 tsp. cinnamon
3 tbsp. agave
1/3 c. raisins

Heat up your oven to 400 degrees and grease a loaf pan. Combine together well the coconut, garbanzo, and quinoa flour with the baking powder and cinnamon. In a separate bowl whisk the eggs with the almond milk and the butter. Once well combined pour in the flour mixture. Beat well until the batter is smooth and has no lumps. Fold in the raisins and it is ready to go into your loaf pan. Bake for 1 hour.

Banana Pancakes with Chocolate Chips

1/3 c. almond flour
2 tbsp. coconut flour
1/4 c. almond milk
3 eggs
1 tsp. vanilla
1 tsp. honey
1/2 tsp. baking soda
1/4 tsp. salt
1 very ripe banana sliced
1/4 c. choc. chips
Butter

Heat up a frying pan over medium to high heat. In a medium bowl mix the flours, baking soda and salt. In a separate bowl beat well the eggs, milk butter, vanilla, and honey. Then slowly mix the flour mixture into the egg mixture. Mix until all lumps are worked out of batter. Let sit for 5 minutes so the flour can soak up additional moisture. Add some butter to your pan and then pour in your first pancake. As the pancake cooks place a few slices of banana on the top and sprinkle chocolate chips in. Flip the pancake over and cook until lightly browned. Then transfer to your plate to enjoy!

Cinnamon Rolls

1/4 c. coconut flour
1 3/4 c almond flour
1/2 tsp. salt
1/4 c. coconut oil
2 tbsp. agave
2 medium eggs
1 tbsp. vanilla

1/4 c agave
2 tbsp. coconut oil
1/4 c. raisins
3 tbsp. cinnamon

1/4 cup pecans (chopped)

Heat your oven up to 350 degrees. Combine the oil, 2 tbsp. agave, eggs and vanilla. In a separate bowl combine the flours and salt until there are no lumps. Mix the two mixtures together and stir well until smooth, then refrigerate for 10 minutes. Next mix 1/4 c agave with 2 tbsp. coconut oil and set aside. Place the dough between two pieces of parchment paper. Take your dough out of the refrigerator and roll it out to form a rectangle. Cover the dough with the oil/agave mixture then cover that with cinnamon and raisins. Start at one end and roll up the dough like a pinwheel. Slice the rolls to the size you would like. We recommend about 2 inches. Line a baking sheet with parchment paper and arrange your rolls on the paper. Bake for about 20 minutes then allow to cool before eating. Then top with chopped pecans.

Blueberry Snack Bars

3/4 c. almond flour
1/2 c. coconut flour
2 tsp. flaxseed
2 eggs
1/2 tsp. cinnamon
1/2 tsp. baking soda
1/4 tsp. salt
1/4 c. butter
1/4 c. honey
1 tsp. vanilla
1 1/2 blueberry preserves
3 tbsp. water

Heat a sauce pan over medium-low heat. Pour in your fruit preserves along with the water. In a medium bowl, mix the flours, flaxseed, cinnamon, salt and baking soda. In a separate large bowl mix together the oil, vanilla, honey and eggs until smooth and creamy. Gradually add the flour mixture into the egg mixture, mixing well as you go. Split the dough in half a roll into two balls. Cover them in plastic wrap and refrigerate for 25 minutes. Remove your preserves and water from the heat and allow to cool down.

Also now is a good time to heat your oven up to 350 degrees and place parchment paper on a baking sheet. Remove the first dough ball from the refrigerator and roll out into a flat disc about 1/4 inch thick. Cut into a large square and then into smaller bar size rectangles (4x2 inches). Next cover each rectangle with blueberry preserves leaving room around the border. Now you remove the second ball of dough from the fridge and repeat roll it out, cut it into a square, and then cut it into smaller rectangles (4x2 inches). Now cover each first piece of dough with preserves. Wet your fingertips and seal around the edges of each bar. Now bake the bars for 12 minutes, then let cool and enjoy the blueberry goodness!

Lemon Dessert Bars

Layer 1:
3/4 c. almond flour
1/4 c. coconut flour
1/2 c. butter
1/2 tsp. salt
Layer 2:
5 eggs
1/2 c. honey
1/2 tsp. baking powder
1/4 tsp. salt
4 tbsp. lemon juice

Heat up your over to 325 degrees and grease a pan (recommended 8x8). Combine the flours, butter, and salt in the Layer 1 ingredients and mix well. Press mixture into pan and bake for 15 minutes until slightly browned. Then mix together until well combined the layer 2 ingredients. Pour over layer 1 and bake for another 15 minutes. Let cool and store in your refrigerator.

Apple Butterscotch Blondies

1/2 c. coconut flour
1 1/2 c. almond flour
2 sticks butter
2 c. brown sugar (light)
2 tbsp. vanilla
1/4 tsp. salt
3 apples diced
1/3 c. butterscotch morsels
1/2 c. walnuts chopped

Heat up oven to 350 degrees and grease a baking dish (9x13). Combine melted butter and brown sugar and dissolve sugar. After that whisk in eggs, salt and vanilla. In a separate bowl combine flours together and then slowly mix into the egg mixture. Once the batter is well blended, fold in apples, walnuts and butterscotch morsels. Pour into baking dish and bake for 35 minutes. Remove from oven and let cool.

Cinnamon Glazed Almond Cookies

1/4 c. coconut flour
2 1/2 c. almond flour
2 eggs
2 tsp. baking powder
1/2 tsp. cinnamon
1/4 c. butter at room temperature
1 tbsp. honey
1 tsp. vanilla extract

Glaze:
2 tbsp. honey
1 tbsp. butter
1 tbsp. cinnamon

Heat up your oven to 350 degrees and line a cookie sheet with parchment paper. In a medium sized mixing bowl sift together the flours, cinnamon and baking soda. Whisk in the eggs, vanilla, honey and 1/4 c. of butter until the smooth dough forms. Roll the dough into 1 inch balls, flatten and line them up on the cookie sheet. Bake for 9 minutes.

While your cookies are baking, combine the glaze ingredients in a bowl and mix thoroughly. After 9 minutes add the glaze to the top of each cookie and bake for an additional 10 minutes. Take the cookies out of the oven and add coconut to the top of the cookies along with an additional layer of glaze. These are delicious and can be enjoyed right away or stored in an airtight Tupper ware for a few days.

Peanut Butter Coconut Cookies

1/4 c. coconut flour
1/2 c. oat flour
1/4 c. almond flour
1/2 c. coconut oil
1 c. peanut butter
1/2 c. honey
1/2 c. sugar
3 eggs
3/4 tsp. vanilla
1/2 tsp. baking soda
1/4 tsp. salt
1/2 c. shredded coconut
1/2 chopped walnuts

Get a large bowl and combine oil, peanut butter, sugar and honey well. Whisk in the 3 eggs, vanilla, baking soda and salt. After everything is combined beat in all three flours, the coconut and the chopped walnuts. Refrigerate the dough for 25 minutes. Heat up your oven to 350 degrees and grease a baking sheet. After the dough has chilled for 25 minutes, roll into balls about 1 inch in diameter. Line them up on the sheet and flatten them out. Bake for 14 minutes and then let cool.

Fruit Cobbler

1/2 tbsp. coconut flour
1 tsp. butter
3 c. cherries
1 c. blueberries
1 diced pear
1 tsp. lemon juice
2 tbsp. honey
1/4 tsp. salt
1.2 tsp. cinnamon

Dough:
2 tbsp. almond flour
1/4 c. coconut flour
1 egg
1/4 tsp. baking soda
1/2 tsp. cinnamon
2 tbsp. butter
1 tbsp. honey
3 tbsp. coconut milk

Heat up your oven to 400 degrees. Heat 1 tsp. of butter over medium heat in a skillet that is oven safe. Add the lemon juice, honey, cinnamon, salt, cherries, blueberries and pears and cook for about 15 minutes. Now add in the 1/2 tbsp. of coconut flour and cook for 1 minute. In a medium bowl combine almond flour, coconut flour, baking soda and cinnamon. In a separate bowl mix the egg, butter, honey and milk. When well combined mix the flour mixture slowly into the egg mixture, dissolving all lumps. Add 1/2 inch flattened balls of the dough on top of the fruit mixture then bake for 12 minutes.

Vanilla Cupcake Recipe

2 tbsp. almond flour
6 tbsp. coconut flour
6 tbsp. butter
5 eggs
1/4 tsp. salt
1/4 cup maple syrup
1/2 tsp. vanilla extract
1/2 tsp. baking powder

Heat up your oven to 400 degrees. Mix together the eggs, vanilla, salt, maple syrup, vanilla and baking powder well. Then stir in the flours and butter. Mix until all lumps are dissolved and batter is smooth. Pour into cupcake liners in a muffin pan and bake for 10 minutes. Frost with your favorite frosting flavor!

IV Coconut and Other Flour Recipes (Without Agave Syrup)

Pigs in a Blanket

2 tbsp. coconut flour
2 c. almond flour
3 tbsp. whey protein powder
2 tsp. baking powder
1/2 tsp. garlic powder
1/2 tsp. salt
2 eggs
1/4 c butter
1 tbsp. butter
3 oz. cheddar cheese
12 hot dogs

Heat your oven up to 350 degrees and line a baking sheet with parchment paper. In a large bowl mix together the flours, protein powder, garlic powder, baking powder and salt. Whisk in eggs and butter until well combined. Place on parchment paper and roll out to 1/4 inch thickness. Cut into a large square and then into 12 smaller squares. Put a hot dog on each square, slice it and sprinkle some cheddar cheese, then roll the square tightly around the hot dog. Brush dough with butter and bake for 20 minutes.

Pizza Crust

3 tbsp. almond flour
1/4 c. coconut flour
1 c. cashew flour
1/2 tsp. baking soda

1/2 tsp. salt
2 eggs
2 tbsp. almond milk
1/2 tsp. vinegar (apple cider)
2 1/2 tbsp. EVOO
1 tbsp. cold water
A pinch parsley
2 tbsp. basil

Heat up your oven to 350 degrees. Fill your food processor with cashews and process them until they are a fine flour. Mix the coconut and almond flours along with the baking soda and salt into the cashew flour and process for 30 more seconds. Next add in the milk, vinegar, EVOO, water and eggs and process for 30 seconds. The dough should be very smooth. Next add the parsley and basil and pulse a few short times. Wait two minutes and then empty the dough out onto a piece of parchment paper sprinkled with almond flour. Sprinkle additional flour on top of the ball and roll it out until it is about 1/4 thick. Bake for about 12 minutes and check for it to turn light brown. Then take it out and top it with your favorite sauce and toppings!

Dinner Rolls

1/4 c. coconut flour
1 c. tapioca flour
1 tsp. salt
1/2 c. water room temperature
1/2 c. olive oil
1 whisked egg

Heat your oven up to 350 degrees and grease a baking sheet. Mix well the two flours together with the salt. Next stir in until well combined the oil, then water, then whisk in the egg. You want the dough to be soft and a little bit sticky. If you want it thicker you can add additional tablespoons of coconut flour. Next you want to make 10 balls of dough containing about 2 tbsp. each. Place the rolls on your baking sheet and bake for 35 minutes.

Pumpkin Blinis

1/2 c. coconut flour
1/3 c. almond flour
1 c. pumpkin puree
1/2 c. parmesan cheese (grated)
1/4 tsp. garlic powder
Pinch of salt
Dash of pepper
1/2 tsp. fresh sage
Butter

Whisk together the eggs, cheese and pumpkin until smooth. In a separate bowl mix the flours, garlic powder, salt, pepper and sage. Combine the two together and mix until smooth. Transfer to the fridge to chill for 15 minutes. Heat a frying pan to medium and melt some butter in it. Remove the dough from the fridge and roll it into 1 inch thick balls. Flatten them out to about 1/2 inch thick and fry in the pan until golden brown on both sides. Serve as an appetizer with toppings such as smoked salmon and sour cream or as a dessert with whipped cream and cinnamon.

Thanks for purchasing this book ! I hope you'll have fun making these recipes. Remember that your health is your biggest asset. Enjoy :)

Recommended Readings

About Coconut Flour :

Aphra, Scarlett, *Coconut Flour Recipes - A Decadent Gluten-Free, Low-Carb Alternative To Wheat*, 2013

Joulwan, Melissa, *Well Fed : Paleo Recipes For People Who Love to Eat*, 2012

Sanflippo, Diane, *Practical Paleo: A Customized Approach to Health and a Whole-Foods Lifestyle*, 2012

Smith, Judy, *Paleo Coconut Flour Recipe Book - A health food transformation guide*, 2013

Wolf, Robb, *Paleo Solution, The Original Human Diet*, 2011

Other Books From the Same Author :

Malet, Cyrille, *Easy Sauerkraut Recipes : Healthy Recipes For Breakfast, Lunch & Dinner*, 2013

Malet, Cyrille, *Getting Healthy with Smoothies : LOSE weight, DETOX your body & BUILD muscle*, 2013

Malet, Cyrille, *70 Easy Budget Recipes - Delicious Recipes That Save You Time & Money*, 2013

Disclaimer

5912159R00020

Printed in Great Britain
by Amazon.co.uk, Ltd.,
Marston Gate.